How To Get Your Grown Woman On

How To Get Your Grown Woman On

Crystal Morris-Newsom, MBA

Edited and Modified By: Carla Jackson-Morris, MAPC

Library of Congress Control Number:		2011903510
ISBN:	Hardcover	978-1-4568-8108-5
	Softcover	978-1-4568-8107-8
	eBook	978-1-4568-8109-2

Print information available on the last page.

Rev. date: 06/13/2022

To order additional copies of this book, contact:
Xlibris
844-714-8691
www.Xlibris.com
Orders@Xlibris.com
589188

Contents

DEDICATION

I dedicate this book to the daughter growing in my womb and to all of the young ladies past, present, and future that can benefit from this book. May your lives be blessed and full of all the hope and promise it should.

Purpose

THE PURPOSE OF this book is to provide a foundation for young girls beginning their journey into womanhood and assist them in understanding the concepts of female development. This book will hopefully support young girls as they experience challenges inside and outside of school. Looking back as a young girl there were so many obstacles that did not support my growth whether it was boys, teachers, or even other girls. We hope this book will help open doors for young girls to connect with their inner thoughts, emotions, feelings, sexual misunderstandings and overall self.

The direction we have chosen for this book is to gradually promote wholeness through the process of imaging, and concepts of what a grown woman is. Does it make a girl grown if she has sex, does drugs, smokes cigarettes, or drinks alcohol? Does it make us cool if we disrespect our parents, dress provocatively, or curse? The way we carry ourselves as women can cloudy the true image of being "grown". We have learned through extensive years of study and real life experiences that young ladies are trying to discover is who they are and why they are who they are. This book will act as a narrator for introducing young girls to a safer and more productive manner in getting their "grown woman on."

To my young ladies reading this book, use it as you journey through junior high and high school to reflect on what you write. This journal can help you through some tough times as a teen girl, so please take the time to write down your thoughts and inner most feelings. After you finish the book, go back over what you have written. You will probably be surprised by what you wrote and it will hopefully help you to learn more about who you are as a young lady and who you want to be. Each day the Lord wakes us up is a new day to make a change. It is never too late!

Image

WHEN YOU LOOK at yourself, who do you see? Do you see a beautiful young girl with a friendly smile, pretty hair, and a cute laugh? Do you see a sexy girl, who can manipulate all of the boys to do what you want them to do? Do you see a tough chick who can whoop another girl's butt and won't let anyone test her? Do you see just a girl, nothing special? Do you see an ugly girl? Do you see a fat girl?

All of these questions have to do with image. I want you to ask yourself this question when you look at yourself in the mirror. "Who do I see in the reflection in the mirror?" Then, I want you to answer the question by saying, "I see (add your name), a beautiful girl that God made only one of in the entire world. That makes me special and I will always be loved by God. I love myself and I love the way I look."

We look at the media and it is fun to check out the music videos of Beyonce, Lady GaGa, Shakira, Nikki Minaj, and all of the other women who parade around with their perfect clothes, perfect cars, perfect face, and perfect bodies. Hey, I am guilty of it myself. I even sometimes think how in the heck can she be pretty all of the time? Don't believe the hype! These women are NOT perfect all of the time. You would be surprised at how much these girls look like you and me without their 12 pounds of make-up on and the digital interference which can remove acne, bruises, blemishes, and stretch marks to make them look perfect; not to mention, the plastic surgery many of them have had to straighten a nose, chin, cheekbone, breast, lips, buttocks, stomach, and anything else on their bodies. Don't be fooled by television. Stars have personal trainers, professional make-up artists, and all sorts of other cosmetic alterations we would never believe that go into making them look the way they do to the public. If you ever catch one of these celebrities without make-up, you will see how much they look just like you and me. Don't base your beauty on famous people because it is all false.

Stars have to put this front up to give us as fans something to WANT to look at. They are selling a puffed up image so we will buy their music, watch their videos, and purchase the type of clothes they wear. It is all about getting us fascinated with them so we will spend money on what they want to sell us. There is absolutely nothing wrong with being beautiful or wanting to look beautiful but I want you to know that natural beauty is just as gorgeous. I can prove it to you. Think about the new commercials we have been seeing about make-up. All of them are trying to sell how natural their brand of make-up feels or looks on the skin. They all tell us that their particular brand will just enhance our natural beauty. Next time you watch television and see one of these commercials listen to what they say. That proves that even make-up companies know the true value and beauty in being natural.

Television is not real no matter how much it seems real. Even on the news, many times we are getting watered down information. This means much of the information we are given is what they want us to have or know not the entire truth. The popularity with reality shows is giving us horrible depictions of women and because they are called "reality" shows we feel it is based on the truth. Wrong! Even the reality shows are false in a lot of ways. We women and young ladies in your case, have to be smart enough to know that these little skinny, perfect chicks on television are not the real deal.

I know you have heard all of this before. You have heard all of the sayings like "beauty is only skin deep," and "everyone is beautiful in their own way." Please ladies listen to me, even though those sayings are annoying they are absolutely 100% the truth. You ARE beautiful in your own way and beauty IS only skin deep. But it's hard to think that when you don't fit the mold of the movie stars or even popular girls in your school. The boys like the girls with the big breasts, long legs, shapely figures, longer hair, thicker make up, and stank attitude. Trust me, let them have that girl because the boy is probably way too shallow to be worth anything anyway. The funny thing is I wish I could let all of you young ladies take a look into my brain to see what I have learned over the years since high school. Many of the girls who were so popular and supposedly so pretty in high school look like crap now and many of the girls that were not considered the prettiest girls in school are gorgeous now. More importantly, the girls that are now gorgeous have an even prettier attitude because they know how it felt not being popular. These are the ladies that have substance and intellect. They are not shallow because they had a brain, heart, and conscience long before they blossomed into beautiful women.

Don't get me wrong, some of the beautiful girls in high school also had substance as well. It wasn't all of the pretty girls that were mean. Sometimes it was the rough unattractive girls that were mean. The main point I want you to understand is no matter where you feel you stand, remember you are beautiful inside and outside so act like it. Be the young lady people will remember as being a nice person with a good heart as well as kind spirit. Work on being a humble and good natured young lady versus being a mean, hateful, vengeful, or envious one. Carrying a humble spirit will also bring you closer to God. Don't forget to remember how wonderful you are as well even in the midst of being humble. To be humble does not mean you have to feel you are inferior but to know how great you are inside and outside. When you realize this you will never have to knock another girl down to feel better about yourself or want to be like anyone else because you will know you are awesome just the way you are. Then use the great young woman you are to help someone else find their greatness.

The boys who like these type of girls much of the time don't respect these girls either, so don't for a second wish to be in their shoes. It hurts to have rumors going around the school about who you slept with. Many times, these same popular girls are talked about in a horrible way in the boys locker room so be thankful for who you are and do not lessen your self respect to be liked by a boy because it will hurt you in the future. If you keep your self respect and dignity, you will attract the RIGHT kind of boy and he will be a keeper!

I want you to write down 3 things that are positive about yourself. Remember there are so many things about you that are unique to only you, whether you play an instrument or sport, are intelligent and make good grades, have a kind heart, have a beautiful smile, have a love for the arts, etc. Write these things down and look at them any time you ever doubt how special you are.

Notes

_____

_____

_____

_____

_____

_____

_____

_____

_____

_____

_____

_____

_____

_____

_____

_____

CRYSTAL MORRIS-NEWSOM, MBA

Notes

_____

_____

_____

_____

_____

_____

_____

_____

_____

_____

_____

_____

_____

_____

_____

_____

_____

_____

Notes

_____

_____

_____

_____

_____

_____

_____

_____

_____

_____

_____

_____

_____

_____

_____

_____

_____

CRYSTAL MORRIS-NEWSOM, MBA

Hygiene

I T'S SIMPLE. JUST bathe every day and you will be fine, right? Wrong! There is much more to hygiene as a female than you would ever expect and I am going to teach you.

First of all, yes you definitely want to make sure you bathe regularly but more than that now that many of you are having menstruation (better known as your "period") you want to make sure you are eating right. Taking baths with bubble bath daily can potentially give you a urinary tract infection so it is best to switch it up and not bathe in the tub every day but to take showers as well. The best thing to drink as a young lady to reduce getting a urinary tract infection is 100% Cranberry Juice and make sure it is 100% juice not 10% juice. If you don't like the taste you can eat Craisins, they taste just like candy. As a last resort, if you don't like the taste of Craisins, you can just purchase Cranberry tablets at any grocery store.

It is so important to maintain a healthy urinary tract. One way you can mess up your urinary tract is by having sex, especially with different boys. Any time you introduce something that isn't clean or is foreign into your body, it can have an adverse effect meaning it can cause you to have an infection. I am hoping that at such a young age you are not having sex because you have your entire life to have sex. However, if you are sexually active be cautious enough to wear a condom no matter what. Sex is very important in life when you have found someone you are in love with and you are of age to wed.

There are many things you can do other than sex that are fun and exciting. Most of the time, if you are thinking of having sex it's because you are being pressured by a boy but you have to be smart. Remember maintain your self respect because having sex to satisfy a boy will not make him respect you. If you say "no" he might leave you to go out with another girl who will have sex with him but the relationship will not last and you won't feel like you lost something. If you have sex with a boy and he breaks up with you, you will feel like he got the best of you. If he breaks up with you and you did not have sex with him, you will feel like at least you still have your virginity and self respect.

It is so important to think about your body as a temple because you don't want some dirty little boy trashing your temple. You can't control how a boy cleans himself or how many girls he has sex with no matter what he says. The only thing you can control is how you protect your body. There are many diseases out there that you can get from having unprotected sex and even if you are protected. The little itchy bugs nicknamed "crabs" are transferred in pubic hair so even if you have on a condom you can still get the bugs in your pubic hair. Yuck! That should be enough reason to wait before having sex.

I don't want to scare you because pubic lice or crabs is very treatable and easy to cure. The main issue is handling the symptoms while you are in the process of treatment such as the horrible itching not to mention having to wash all of your clothes over again even the clean clothes, bed sheets, couch covers, pillows, rugs in some cases, and any other cloth-like material that might have been exposed to the bugs. If you don't get everything washed you can potentially infect yourself again and have to start the process all over again. However, I want you to be educated on your body and your health. Pay attention to your body, it will tell you everything you need to know about it. The symptoms of a urinary tract infection are pain in your stomach or lower abdominal area and sometimes in your lower back if your bladder is affected. There is also irritation, pain, or urgency during urination/peeing. Sometimes your urine can smell very strong and burn when you go to the restroom.

To add to the topic of menstruation, there a few tips that every young girl needs to know. Some of you may already know these things from your mother, sister, or grandmother but if you didn't have this talk with one of them now you will have the information at your disposal. If you use pads make sure you always wrap them up with the pad's wrapper or roll it up and wrap toilet paper around it before discarding it in the garbage can. Try

CRYSTAL MORRIS-NEWSOM, MBA

to keep a couple of back-up pads/tampons in your purse in case you begin your period early and keep extras during your period so you have enough to get you through a school day. Don't keep the same pad or tampon on for more than a few hours even if you're at the end of your period and your flow is light. If you keep it on for too long it might make you have a bit of an odor that isn't very pleasant and can be embarrassing. Make sure you are showering more regularly just to make you feel confident and stay fresh. For instance, if you normally bathe once per day, during your period add an extra shower per day to your routine. Another thing to remember is to shower only while menstruating versus taking a bath. If you want to be as fresh as possible taking a bath will not help you achieve that result since you will be sitting in dirty water. Menstruating is a beautiful part of being female even though it can be a nuisance. It also comes with great responsibility because now you are capable of getting pregnant. Take care of yourself inside and out because if you want to get your grown woman on you must do both.

Hygiene has everything to do with your body and how you treat it. You have to try to maintain the body you have been blessed with. Hey, you only get one body ladies. Always wash your face and keep your teeth brushed each morning and at night. Keep your nails clean and your hands washed with antibacterial soap. This will also help decrease the number of times you get sick in a school year. It is important to know how to care for your own body because you might have a daughter some day (hopefully after college and marriage) that you need to teach how to get her grown woman on.

You are the only one who can protect your body so take care of it and if you need assistance with anything you can do a search online to find out the answers. You can enter in symptoms and it will tell you potential diagnoses of what you might have. Boys think of themselves for the most part, it is time for young ladies to think of themselves as well. It's not all about the boys and what they want, what about what you want? You want a healthy urinary tract, disease free body, and respectful image, right? Well stand by your principles. If the boy cares he will be there for you still until you are ready to take it to that other level but please don't be persuaded by a smooth talking boy who is only thinking with his body parts.

Take some time to think about ways you can enhance your hygiene, write down 3 things you can do:

Notes

CRYSTAL MORRIS-NEWSOM, MBA

Notes

_____

_____

_____

_____

_____

_____

_____

_____

_____

_____

_____

_____

_____

_____

_____

_____

_____

_____

Notes

_____

_____

_____

_____

_____

_____

_____

_____

_____

_____

_____

_____

_____

_____

_____

_____

_____

CRYSTAL MORRIS-NEWSOM, MBA

Doesn't it feel good to take the time to focus on you as a young lady? It is fun to learn about ourselves and start making goals for ourselves. If we don't have a game plan on how we are going to carry ourselves than it is very easy to lose sight of who we are and what we want out of life.

Familial Relationships

IN TODAY'S SOCIETY, we have become such a "microwave population." We don't sit at the kitchen table to eat dinner together as a family and we don't have family meetings to discuss family issues anymore. Unfortunately, our youth is being raised by television and peers because we just don't have the time to take with our kids. This is unacceptable but understandable. There are many single parent households which makes it tough financially so they have to work even harder to make ends meet." This is not a BAD thing so please don't carry hostility or hold grudges against your parents for trying to make a living to support you. Trust me, there are many parents who put their own selfish wants above their children's needs versus trying to provide for their children.

On the other hand, if you do in fact have a parent who is rather selfish and doesn't show you the love or attention you feel you need or you happen to be in a single parent household, the worst possible thing you can do is look for what you're missing in a boy. If you truly need love, friendship, or someone to talk to, the best thing you can do is join a church. Most churches have youth programs that provide an abundance of love and support to teens plus it will show you that there is a higher being that loves you more than words could ever express and that is God. It is very disheartening for me to see a young girl whose parent(s) have failed her but the only people we can change or correct is ourselves, no matter how bad we want too. There are many other productive ways you can seek help and companionship.

I met a girl at church when I was a young mother around 21 years of age. She was also a young mother but in her late teens and with multiple children. It was much harder for her than it was for me with my one son. I used to admire how she was always at church every Sunday with her three children and I couldn't imagine how hard it must have been on her. It might have been tough but she chose to pursue a positive lifestyle even if it was tough. We used to talk about life. She would explain how she had no help because the children's father was in jail and both of her parents were on drugs. She had no other family at all except her precious children. Eventually, through prayer and diligence she was able to get a really good job from another lady in the church and her life was changed. Never think that all hope is gone in your life no matter what your family situation is because God has a plan for all of us. Make the best of whatever parents you have and forgive them for any indiscretions they may have made. I know it's tough to forgive people when they hurt you but when you forgive them it actually releases a weight from your shoulders and gives you peace to move on with your life successfully.

I have found that many times in situations where a parent is selfish, abusive, nonchalant, or unnecessarily mean to their children it is because they don't know any better. Much of the time they were raised that way, so they don't really know any other way to behave. Don't think for a second that your precious grandma or grandpa couldn't have been that mean or abusive to your parent because being a parent is different than being a grandparent. It's like the old saying which says that "hindsight is 20/20". It means that it is easier to see what mistakes you made and how you should have been after it's already happened and you are looking back at it. The picture is much clearer once you look back over your life but most of the time it is too late to change what happened. I am not, I repeat NOT making excuses for anyone but when you understand a situation you can live with it better whether it is right or wrong. You young ladies need to know that you are a treasure and even if your parent doesn't show it very well they love you deep down inside.

Use the time you have as a young lady to make yourself the best you can be by getting into extracurricular activities such as sports, clubs, and church organizations to fill the void you might be feeling. Again, this is very important please do not try to fill the void from your parents by getting into an intimate relationship with a boy. It will actually give you an even bigger void in the end. I know it's hard to think of breaking up with a boy when you are so in love with him or so you think but don't make decisions based on how you feel.

CRYSTAL MORRIS-NEWSOM, MBA

I know you are intelligent because God is intelligent and He made us all in his own image. We all have the ability to think so USE YOUR BRAIN! Don't choose to ignore signs that a boy is bad news just because you want to make your parents mad or so you can feel a sense of security. At this stage in your life, it will only hurt you in the end and make you feel insecure. This is your time to get to know yourself and have fun. Yes, boys can be fun but as soon as you begin having sex your life takes on another level of responsibility. You have to think about the young girl I met at church and how hard her life was with three children at a young age. I know she loves her beautiful children but what she wouldn't have given just to be a real teenager versus a teenage mom. There was no going to the movies, going on dates, going to high school dances, and proms for my friend at church. She had to work and try to provide for her children. She got her grown woman on, but much too early. I want you to get your grown woman on but in steps. There is no rush to be a woman because most of your life will be lived as an adult so enjoy being a teenager. You have to know that you were made in the image of the most high. The only way you will be respected is to keep your legs closed and open your minds to understand what it really means to be grown.

To be grown means being responsible with not only your house key, cellular phone, or allowance but also your bodies. At what cost will you as a young girl have to pay in order to speed up the process of getting to womanhood? Meaning what part of your wonderful self will you have to sacrifice to be grown before your time? Do not use any excuses as you live your life even if you have issues with your parents or siblings. Whatever you do keep your temper at a minimum and always respect elders. The Bible mentions how important it is to be obedient to your parents. It goes as far as to say that if children are not obedient they will not live long lives. Please talk to a social worker or counselor at school or again at your church to get help in dealing with your issues with your parents. But if you need to know more about what it means to take care of the beautiful young lady you are let this book start to help. It will only hurt you, if you do not get help. This is the time to write out your feelings and talk about it. Find another way to work through your hurt and pain instead of doing things that ultimately hurt yourself when it's all said and done. Prove it to yourself that you can do it and you can be anything that you want to be in this world. We now have an extraordinary African American man who is president of the United States and who knows you might be the first woman to be president. It doesn't matter where you came from, just focus your mind on where you are going, and want to go in this life. Isn't it an exciting thought? Just think of all the opportunities you have and it can truly happen for you. Whatever our mothers teach us or show us in their actions doesn't mean we accept it into our hearts if it's not positive. Let this book free your mind and soul to be the beautiful queens that God made you to be.

Write down any issues or areas of pain that you feel with regard to your mother and/or father. Next write down why you think your mother and/or father treats you this way or acts like this. For example, think about how your parents were raised by your grandparents and things that might have happened to your parents growing up. Now the last step is very important, and please make sure you complete all of the steps in this chapter. Use the very last line to write, "I forgive you mom and I love you," or "I forgive you dad and I love you."

In this chapter, I want you to feel cleansed. I want you to feel brand new. When you write things down it helps you to release negative things into the atmosphere so you don't have to be weighed down by them. If you were honest in this step and wrote about the things done by your parents that truly hurt you, why they might have done it, and then forgive them for it . . . you will gain an insurmountable amount of strength, courage, and determination in your life. When you can try to understand what is going on in your life and then release it you gain insight and hence mature towards "getting your grown woman on." Many times parents do hurtful things because of their own fear, unhappiness or insecurities so don't take offense just try to understand and move past it. Don't let negative things come inside your temple and spoil the great young lady God has intended for you to be. It doesn't matter who is trying to kill and steal your joy just don't let it happen.

When you write things down it takes the weight off of your shoulders so you can release it into the atmosphere. So even if you don't talk to anyone about your issues you will feel as though you did because you got it off of your chest. The forgiveness part is an important step because when you forgive them for whatever it is you feel like they have done, you will be able to love yourself more efficiently. Now that you understand where the issues come from, you can better handle them, versus feeling out of control and helpless.

CRYSTAL MORRIS-NEWSOM, MBA

Notes

_____

_____

_____

_____

_____

_____

_____

_____

_____

_____

_____

_____

_____

_____

_____

_____

_____

Notes

CRYSTAL MORRIS-NEWSOM, MBA

Notes

_____

_____

_____

_____

_____

_____

_____

_____

_____

_____

_____

_____

_____

_____

_____

_____

_____

Dating

THERE WAS A time back in the day when young boys would actually court a young lady. When a young man would court or date a young woman he would bring her flowers, write her letters, open doors for her at school, hold her books, and walk her to her classes. If the young man and woman were old enough, he would ask her parents for permission to date her. Wow, I know this seems hard to believe but this is how my grandparents were raised. My grandfather pursued my grandmother and asked her mother for permission to date her. He then asked for her hand in marriage shortly thereafter. My grandparents have been married for over 50 years and when I look at them I am reminded of the beautiful way in which dating occurred. By the way, if you are under 16 years of age then you probably shouldn't be dating anyway. However, if your parents have allowed you to date than you should at least try to date the best candidate. Besides aren't you a wonderful young woman? If you truly believe that, than you know that you deserve a wonderful young man.

Although many young men would laugh at the mention of how dating used to commence, there are still some young men who were raised to use some of these dating values. Whatever the case may be, you are in control of how you will be treated by a young man. Only you can put forth what you will and will not accept from a young man. If you think it sounds nice to date a young man who talks disrespectfully to you, walks in front of you, treats you like you are nothing to him, puts his friends in front of you, and makes you feel worthless than it is your choice to be with him. But think about how great it would feel being the center of a young man's attention. You wouldn't even have to guess if he cares about you because he would show it in how he treats you by the respect he shows you. He talks to you like a lady and wants nothing but the best for you. I'm sure the "bad boy" will tell you he cares about you but you have to learn that the best way to know if a young man cares about you is by how he treats you. Never take only a young man's word. Make sure the words are accompanied by positive actions.

Here are a couple of signs to look for as you get to the age of dating or as you are already experiencing dating. One sign to always look for in a young man is how he treats his sister(s) and mother. If he is very belligerent and disrespectful to his mother and sisters than chances are, he will be belligerent and disrespectful to you. Think about it, at your age who could be more important to him than his own mother and sister? If he can't respect them than he probably won't be able to respect you because he doesn't know how and you can't teach him. Another sign is if he "goes for bad." I know "bad boys" seem exciting to young ladies because they are so mysterious but they will also break your heart. Always remember that a young man is who he is and there is nothing you can do to change him into who you want him to be. I know women who thought they could change a man that they were dating who was a "bad boy". Ten years later the man is the exact same way he was as the first day she met him.

Don't waste your time with a young man who will treat you less than you deserve. This next sign seems like common sense but I want to still mention it because it is definitely happening. If a young man is ditching school than he is not going down the right path. School is an integral part of a young man and young woman's life. It is your main responsibility as a child and teenager to complete school. The better grades you make in school the better the next step becomes for you. In high school, the better your grades are, the more money you will receive from scholarships to attend college. Scholarships are free money to those who earn it so don't waste your time with a young man who does not have the same drive and motivation to become something in life. A young man like that, can only bring you down to his level versus you soaring to the highest of heights in your life. Along the same lines, do not even consider dating a man who is doing drugs whether it is smoking marijuana or drinking alcohol. This is an obvious sign that he is not going down a positive path however again it needs to be addressed because far too many young girls date these types of young men expecting to change him. Last but not least, please do not think getting involved with a gangbanger is cool because it is not only dangerous but a huge sign that he will not be a good young man to date. Being

CRYSTAL MORRIS-NEWSOM, MBA

with a gangbanger might provide you with a sense of security because he acts so tough all of the time. However, think about this part of the whole gangbanger mentality and lifestyle. A gangbanger has to be true to his gang first and foremost which means you will be pushed to the back burner and that is not a fun position to be in. The lifestyle usually calls for drug selling, drug using, stealing, and even murder so who in their right mind would want to begin dating someone who will most likely be in prison soon. I am not judging them and I am definitely not wishing bad luck on these young boys who unfortunately feel gangs are the answer. My primary objective is to save young women so I have to be single minded and focus on you.

I want to clarify some things for you young women because it is so important that you understand that you are not the first young lady to experience what you are experiencing. Even though you think adult women don't understand where you are coming from, we do. When I tell you to stay clear of the young men I have mentioned, I am not saying that these young men don't have good hearts. They could have great hearts but the only thing you can do for them is pray for them and move on unless you are willing to sacrifice yourself, your family, and your future for these boys. If you are willing to make such a huge sacrifice for a young man than that is your choice. However, in a real relationship it is never one person making all of the sacrifice. In a loving relationship with two people on the same level, each of the parties have to make sacrifices to be with one another.

To clarify even further, a sacrifice is something that is done out of love not out of control. Don't be fooled by a young man who says a sacrifice is not having girlfriends other than you, or I didn't go steal that car because of you. That is not a sacrifice that is just doing the right thing. I have been in your shoes. I have dated a young man who even though he was a thug, did drugs, and even hit me I still held on to the small number of good times we had. I would think in my naïve head, I know he loves me and has a good heart, he just has to get himself together and I will help him do it. I would believe all of his sad stories about how unfair life had been for him which made me want to rescue him. Listen, it is not your responsibility to rescue anyone but yourself. It might sound harsh but it is the truth. You are only a young woman and the only one who can rescue a young man like that is God so do both of you a favor and pray for him but leave him alone. To this day, the young boy I dated decades ago is now a grown man still doing the same thing he was doing when I left him. If I stayed with him, I am positive I would be living a life of negativity and regret. You have to learn from other women's mistakes because you don't want to waste your time or energy on a young man who is not worthy.

I wish I would have listened to my mother but I was just like you. I thought my mother didn't understand what I was going through so I had to learn the hard way. It almost sounds insane to me now that instead of listening to my mother I would rather experience all of that hurt, pain, and abuse myself. That is like saying, "Please someone just take out a bat and hit me over the head because I like pain." I want a better life for you than I had and I'm sure your parents want the same thing. My children are my world and I talk to them about things I have been through so they can hopefully avoid making some of the same mistakes I have made hence making their life much easier than mine. I brought many things on myself by being hard headed and not listening to my mother. Be smarter than I was and take heed to the signs in a young boy who is showing you interest to see if he is worth you dating versus just accepting the first boy who shows you any interest. You have the right to be choosey in who you date because remember God made you special and there is not one other person in this world like you (unless you're a twin). That means there is a young man out there that God made just for you and God will bring him into your life when the time is right. If you determine the boy you are dating is disrespectful, and any of the other signs I mentioned; run away fast.

If you are not of age to date, I want you to write down as many things you can think of that represents a nice young man who is worthy of you dating. I want you to be honest and I want you to always think about these things as you mature.

If you are already dating, I want you to write down the boy's name(s) and then make a T-chart. A T-chart is a list of the good and bad things about each boy. (Be honest because if you are not, the only person you are hurting is yourself). After you complete your T-chart on each candidate, compare to see which boy has more bad than good and these are the boys to cross out. There is not one young man or young woman for that matter in the world who is perfect but you don't want to be around anyone who has more negative traits than good traits. If the T-chart shows that the young man has an equal amount of good and bad traits than cross his name out as well. Remember you are a wonderful princess who deserves a prince. What

CRYSTAL MORRIS-NEWSOM, MBA

you need to be looking for is the young man who has the majority of his traits on the good side and a small amount of bad traits.

Of course, all of this writing is about boys who did not have the signs I have already mentioned because all of those signs are deal breakers. No matter if he has a million good traits, if he ditches school, smokes, does drugs, and is a gangbanger he is not worth your time. If you begin focusing on yourself more, you will find that you don't have time to find boys but eventually the RIGHT boy will find you.

Notes

_____

_____

_____

_____

_____

_____

_____

_____

_____

_____

_____

_____

_____

_____

_____

_____

_____

CRYSTAL MORRIS-NEWSOM, MBA

Notes

Notes

_____

_____

_____

_____

_____

_____

_____

_____

_____

_____

_____

_____

_____

_____

_____

_____

CRYSTAL MORRIS-NEWSOM, MBA

Gossip

I REMEMBER HIGH school like it was yesterday. I remember the jock girls, the cheerleaders, the popular girls, nerds, and the not so popular girls. I think I was a mixture between the jock girls, nerds, and popular girls but I always spent time with the unpopular girls because I had honors classes with them.

I was a science geek that played basketball and liked to dress fashionably. I had a combination because of my mom's raising. I was in shape and my frame matured early so I had an older body for a girl my age. All of the girls that were jocks like me were nice to me to my face and during the season but not during the off-season. Many of the older basketball girls acted like they hated me for no reason at all. I always thought it had to be because they all wore "boy" clothes and acted like boys. I, on the other hand wore fashionable "girl" clothes and acted like a girl. I dated a guy off campus who was older than me which now I realize was definitely a mistake, although I was mature for my age. Much of my childhood was lost dating that older guy because I was too busy trying to be older than I was to make him happy. I regret losing that time but can never get it back. That is why I'm writing to you because you have the opportunity to learn from some of my mistakes and live a better life than I lived. Back to my days playing basketball, I guess I never really fit with the jock girls because of those reasons however, I loved basketball. I just didn't feel I had to act and look like a boy to be a ball player.

As a nerd, although I loved science and enjoyed my honors classes my attire always seemed to be on the sexy side for a nerd so some of my instructors pre-judged me until they got to know me. To clarify, my clothes were tasteful but because my friends and I were very shapely girls for our age we looked different in our clothes then other girls our age. I had one instructor who was dead set on proving I was an airhead and kept trying to flunk me by having me retake tests in Physics honors but I kept passing them. He went so far as to try to prevent me from graduating high school. He waited until the week of graduation to tell me I had to retake the first exam from the school year because he couldn't find any record of it (even though I had already taken it). If I didn't pass the exam, he said he would fail me and I would not be able to graduate. My mom went to the school with me, I retook the test and passed it. My mother's support coupled with God's grace got me through it. It hurts me to see that not all young girls have the love and support my mom gave me. That is exactly why I want to try to show as much love and concern for you as I possibly can through this book whether you are receiving it at home or not.

I had my own set of friends who I had grown up with since kindergarten. I didn't feel I had to fit in with everyone else because I was blessed to go to school with them which sort of made us popular. We were our own little clique and we loved to dress. We also loved setting new trends by wearing things that nobody at the school wore. We prided ourselves on our clothes and we got a lot of attention from the boys because of it. The attention came with a price because some of the boys at the school started rumors about us. We made it through the rumors because we had each other to depend on. Some of the rumors really hurt but we made it through high school by sharing our pain with one another.

Now that you have a little background information, you can understand how gossip started to spread about us. We used to hear gossip about us being stuck up because we only hung around each other or rumors regarding us sleeping with this guy or that guy. We were far from stuck up, we just didn't want to be alone so we clung to one another. Create a network of friends to lean on because it offers much support. After school I would go home and get pep talks from my mother and grandmother who both went through the same issues as a teen. Even though they are from two totally different generations they still experienced everything I was going through.

One of the most hurtful things that can happen to a girl is to be talked about falsely. If you happen to be going through some of this same stuff, I feel your pain. Just know that gossip means you must be a heckuva bombshell or something for them to have your name in their mouth. Nowadays, they call it "hating." Well let people hate on you all they want, just know that it is their own insecurities that drive them to hate on you because they evidently envy something about you. Trust me, I know you have more going on for yourself than even YOU think. You have to stay encouraged and know that the gossip will pass and you will still be the great young lady that you are. All young women have to experience a little bit of gossip in their life here and there. High school is the perfect breeding ground for gossip because girls get so jealous of each other.

If you are reading this book and you know that you are spreading a hurtful rumor about another girl you don't like please CUT IT OUT! It will come to bite you in the butt and I'm telling you to put yourself in their shoes. Even if you think the rumor is true, don't judge them because none of us are perfect and you are not God so you can't judge them. Young ladies have to stop spreading hurtful rumors and gossip around about people because even if someone acts like it doesn't hurt them at school, some girls will go home and cry all night. Gossip affects some girls so much that they change schools or just drop out of school altogether. Just be nice and friendly to each other because karma can be ugly. If you keep trying to hurt others, it will come back on you harsher. I know you are not going to like everyone you come into contact with but if you don't like them stay away from them. You don't have to bad mouth the person's name for any reason. It is cruel and ugly to intentionally hurt someone's feelings, so please young ladies work on not gossiping about each other. There is healthy gossip. With the millions of reality shows on, you can gossip with each other. You can gossip about American Idol, Dancing With The Stars, or even celebrities but not each other because it hurts so bad.

If you have spread an untrue story about another female please write down what you said. Then I want you to write down how you would feel if an untrue story was spread about you. If you spread gossip about another girl but you feel the story is true, I want you to think about a mistake you have made in your life that you would hate for someone to spread all over the school. If you don't feel you have ever made a mistake that you wouldn't want someone to find out about, then think of the most embarrassing moment you have ever had and if someone were to share that with the entire school. Now write down the mistake or embarrassing moment and how you would feel if it were spread all over the school. Last, I want you to ask for forgiveness by just saying Lord I am sorry for what I have done and ask that you forgive me in the name of Jesus.

Notes

CRYSTAL MORRIS-NEWSOM, MBA

Notes

_____

_____

_____

_____

_____

_____

_____

_____

_____

_____

_____

_____

_____

_____

_____

_____

Notes

_____

_____

_____

_____

_____

_____

_____

_____

_____

_____

_____

_____

_____

_____

_____

_____

CRYSTAL MORRIS-NEWSOM, MBA

Thoughts of Suicide

SUICIDE IS A very serious subject for teens in today's society. There is a lot of pressure for our young ladies especially with television making them think you have to be a Barbie doll in order to be beautiful. Boy's attitudes have drastically changed as well due to the vulgarity of language and the lack of respect and values being taught in the home. I have heard boys talk to young girls in such derogatory terms that it has made my stomach turn. I have heard them call young girls whores or the "b" word more times than I care to admit. These are only words but they hurt. I know this first hand because I have been called mean names before. But I'm here to tell you that words are only skin deep. Words do not define who you are as a young lady no matter what you have been through in life and no matter what mistakes you may have made.

Boys lack this respect because it is so accepted in our world today. There was a time when boys actually treated young ladies and even elders with respect. They greeted elders with "Mr." or "Mrs." and offered to help them with their groceries. You don't have to be like everyone else and you definitely do not have to be like television. God has given us joy and love in our hearts so we should share it with everyone around us. We are not deserving of what God does for us. Remember not to let people steal the joy and love that God has blessed you with even if they treat you badly. Each morning that God wakes you up provides you with a brand new opportunity to better your life and get past the worst of situations. Don't ever feel as though you are not worth anything to anyone because you are worth so much to God and you are worth a lot to me or I wouldn't be writing this book for you. I don't want you to injure yourself in any way because I know that you can be great in this world. You have to have faith that God will pull you through whatever obstacles that you encounter.

Did you know that suicide is the 3rd leading cause of death for 15-24 year olds and the 6th leading cause of death for 5-14 year olds according to American Academy of Child and Adolescent Psychiatry? Girls attempt suicide twice as much as boys. That means that more young girls are attempting suicide than boys are. These statistics are heartbreaking since I understand the issues we face as young and old women. But again, it is not worth going to hell or hurting the people who love us. The Bible says it is a sin to commit suicide and it makes sense when you think about it. God made us so how dare we feel as though we can decide when we are done living this life. It is not our choice to make, it is God's choice to make.

There are many reasons young women feel they should commit suicide and I want to address them because I want you to see that what you are going through is not new. Most of us have experienced one or more of these issues. Issues like having a breakup with your boyfriend, your parents going through a divorce, something traumatic happening like a parent dying, loved one dying, getting pregnant, gaining weight, being raped, and the list goes on.

As you experience one or more of these issues you might begin to feel depressed, unusually tired, angry, or you might want to start using drugs/alcohol. It is okay to feel sad but do not wallow in your situation because it is unhealthy and never turn to drugs. The best thing to do is force yourself to get up and go for a walk to admire the beauty of God's earth. Take deep breaths, listen to the birds, pick flowers, cry, and please pray for God to strengthen you to get past your situation. Taking the time to talk with a friend, parent, family member, school teacher, counselor, or pastor is a great way to release how you're feeling as well. Whatever you do, do not keep it bottled inside of you because it can make you ill. You have to get it out somehow. Even using this book to write about what is bothering you and how you feel about it is a great release.

At a young age I was molested by a 40 year old man. If it weren't for the acknowledgement, understanding, and validation from my mother to reassure me it wasn't my fault, I might have experienced some depression and feelings of worthlessness. She told me I was still special and that he didn't steal my innocence. When someone takes advantage of you in that way, it makes you feel cheap and worthless. It makes you feel as though you are to blame for what happened to you. You begin to think that you

deserved it because of what you wore or what you did. I am here to tell you that whether it's a young boy or an older man, it is ALWAYS wrong for him to force himself on you. He might have a problem which means he has probably done it to someone else or will do it to someone else so tell someone you trust to gain support and then call the police so it doesn't happen again.

There is a phenomenon that has been around for decades but now it has a title. It is called, "date rape". This is something that can happen by your boyfriend, close friend, or even just a first date. Here is a scenario; you are out on a date in an empty movie theater watching the newest movie. All of a sudden, your boyfriend reaches over to kiss you and you kiss him back. Now you two are making out in the movie theater. After a minute or two you move your head back and tell him you want to finish watching the movie but he tells you to stop playing hard to get. He starts kissing you again but with much more aggression and now he is trying to put his hands under your skirt. You tell him to stop but he just keeps going and as you try to fight him off. He holds you down and forces you to have sex with him. A couple of things I want to mention before I discuss how this is rape. Remember this is just a scenario, so if your event is different it doesn't mean it's your fault. For instance, if you two were making out for ten minutes versus only two minutes, if you let him put his hands under your skirt or shirt, or any other details it still doesn't give him the right to force himself on you. If you aren't sure your situation was rape, then ask yourself these two questions. Did I tell him to stop? Did he make me have sex with him by force? If these two things happened then you were raped.

Now, I am going to add to this topic for the manipulative little girls who think it's cute to cry wolf. I know you would never do this but this paragraph is solely for the girls who might read this book who like to play games to get back at boys. Lying about being raped is very serious and you can go to jail for filing a false report so there are consequences. If a boy dumps you, you shouldn't try to ruin his life by lying about him raping you. That is one of the worse things you can do is to put an innocent boy in jail. If it happens to be a mother reading this book who has a son as well as a daughter don't hesitate to press charges to the full extent of the law. I have two boys myself and I don't do very well with games, so I would definitely file charges against a girl who lied on my son about raping her. It is one of

the lowest things a young girl can do and definitely isn't getting your grown woman on. A "grown" woman would never allow herself to be so low as to put someone in jail falsely. Never cry wolf because it is so true that people will not believe you if something really does happen to you.

"A word to parents on the subject of suicide from Carla Jackson-Morris, MAPC, a professional counselor in Arizona and author of "Just Hold On: Overcoming Private Emotions of Fear":

According to the U.S. Suicide Statistics, the highest suicide rates in America stem from the elderly and younger populations. In the older population the feelings of despair from being forgotten are pushing them to suicidal thoughts and oddly enough it is the same for the youth, who also feel forgotten. Suicide is the eleventh leading cause of death for all Americans.

"As stable adults, we have to realize that if the world seems complicated and unbearable to us, we can just imagine how our children feel. We have to know that not believing in a higher power, and carrying overwhelming uncertainties by ourselves without the help of God will lead to suicidal thoughts. If we are not taught or educated on the premise that God is our higher power and that we can always take our problems to Him, it will be easy for our children to feel lost in this world. The youth is left feeling there is no purpose in life due to the lack of divine intervention. The Bible tells us that there will be storms however without the understanding of God we will not pass through the storm, but get trapped in it. Suicidal thoughts are fears unleashed. There are many fears teenagers face such as not being liked, accepted, understood, or appreciated. Adults have to teach our young that they will have these storms and in order to push through them they will need the shield and armor of their higher power for protection. These children need to know that they cannot do it alone, and thanks be to God they do not have to do it alone because God is always with them even when we do not deserve it. It is okay to ask for help and our young ladies have to learn how to ask for help, talk about their problems, and most of all know that there is a gangster that is truly a conqueror of all, and his name is Jesus Christ. We must empower our young ladies to be conquerors, to weather the storm, and then pass through it."

If you have gone through a traumatic experience, it's time to release it into the atmosphere so that it can never weigh you down again. I want you

take the time to write down what happened to you. Go into detail because this is your personal journal to yourself and nobody has to read it. Write how the experience made you feel at the time and how you are currently feeling. Then say out loud, "I cannot change the past but I can live today as a happy young lady leaving my past behind me." Now I want you to write that sentence down. The last thing I want you to do is say out loud, "it was not my fault." The last sentence in this chapter should say in upper case letters, "IT WAS NOT MY FAULT."

You should feel some immediate relief but don't think this will be all you need to do to get over this tough time. You will still need to pray continually and find comfort in another positive person such as a youth pastor, pastor, counselor, teacher, mother, or father. There are people who will help you so please do not feel as though you have to get through this alone.

Notes

CRYSTAL MORRIS-NEWSOM, MBA

Notes

_____

_____

_____

_____

_____

_____

_____

_____

_____

_____

_____

_____

_____

_____

_____

_____

Notes

CRYSTAL MORRIS-NEWSOM, MBA

Alcoholism and Drugs

DRINKING ALCOHOL AND smoking marijuana with your friends is exciting to many of the youth today. It is fun to break the rules sometimes and live a little dangerously. Many adults (maybe even your parents) have experimented with alcohol, drugs, or both however times are different today than back then. Teenagers today are much more in tune with what is going on in the world through the internet, television, and even school. Back in the day, it was taboo to discuss drugs in school. Equally different today, there are many other dangers that us adults didn't have to face back in our day. Now there are pills such as ecstasy and other scary drugs out there like Meth that is hurting our beautiful young girls. We cannot become a society of no feel, no thrill, unless we've got a pill. Come on ladies! We have to be strong and think. If we do drugs it makes our complexion bad, breath stink, and drug users tend to look disheveled or messy after doing drugs. We can't make good decisions as young ladies under the influence of drugs.

It is sad when I meet someone who I went to school with who was a beautiful girl in elementary school and everyone wished they were her but she is now on drugs. The girl looks totally different. Replacing her glowing smile is rotted out teeth, replacing her great figure is a skinny little frame, and replacing her great skin is spotted, scaly, damaged skin that looks like it can rip right off of her face. But, I know of course it could NEVER happen to you because you are way too smart to get addicted to drugs. Please listen to me because I know what I'm talking about. I am not only writing about it, I lived it through many of my good friends and family who are now dead or in the streets because of drugs. These are not just average people but extremely intelligent people with extraordinary skills and talents. It CAN happen to you, if you allow yourself to become wrapped up in drugs or alcohol. Some people can get addicted after just trying it one time so please don't think you are immune to it. Drugs are chemicals so they can totally alter the mental processes in your brain and MAKE you crave them. It can happen to ME, if I allow myself to fall into that trap. No matter the reason, drugs and alcohol are bad for your body, mind, soul, and spirit.

Remember you are a beautiful young lady who is going to uphold herself as a little lady or else you will be treated according to your actions. My mom would always tell me, "Don't let your good be evil spoken." All the saying means is to present yourself like a lady because sometimes you can look like a certain type of person such as an "easy" girl and inside be a "good" girl. This misrepresentation occurs a lot in today's society with the television providing our young girls with the latest fashions that are rather risqué as well as the sexiest commercials for alcohol. If you don't want nasty old men to salivate at you when you walk by, wear a skirt that doesn't show the bottom of your buttocks and definitely not be drunk or under the influence of drugs. Of course, if there is a nasty old man out there, he might make goo goo eyes at you even if you had on your grandmother's sweater with an ankle length skirt. Either way, be sure to represent yourself as a lady and not become intoxicated because if your judgment is impaired it will be hard to protect yourself from making bad decisions such as wearing protection during sex, paying attention to your surroundings and unwanted attention, and from achieving your dreams.

I don't want to scare you but there are many sexual predators out there waiting for a young girl just like you to make one fatal mistake. You go to a party and get wasted only to find that you are actually being stalked by someone with bad intentions. It is sad but you have to protect yourself as a young lady because you just never know when you might need your brilliant mind at peak performance to get you out of danger. You really can be all you desire to be in this world but it starts now with making smart choices. You can be a singer like Beyonce, a tennis player like Venus and Serena, a race car driver like Mia Hamm, a judge like Sotomayor, a talk show host or model like Tyra, a movie star like Halle Berry, a minister like Joyce Meyer, and the list goes on. Your entire life is based upon the choices you make now. Please don't get worried I know you will make mistakes because we all do but just know deep down inside that even if you falter your steps you can dust yourself off and continue on your journey.

Take the time to write down all of your goals and dreams. Then I want you to write down how drugs and alcohol can prevent you from achieving these goals and dreams.

Notes

CRYSTAL MORRIS-NEWSOM, MBA

Notes

_____

_____

_____

_____

_____

_____

_____

_____

_____

_____

_____

_____

_____

_____

_____

_____

Notes

CRYSTAL MORRIS-NEWSOM, MBA

Last Word From The Author

AS YOU MATURE from a young lady to "getting your grown woman on" you will have some obstacles to overcome. I want you to know that whatever comes in your life to falter your steps or stop you from reaching your goals and aspirations you can pray it away. Ask the Lord to remove anything negative from your life in the name of Jesus. There is no perfect life and there is no perfect mixture of ingredients that will make life simple. However, you can lessen confusion and pain in your life by opening your heart and mind to learning from the mistakes of others who have gone through this journey before you like myself and your parents. It might have been a different year that we were going through it but trust me we all face the same issues.

Know that you are a beautiful princess that is blossoming into a queen. You deserve a king to put you on a pedestal and treat you special. Likewise, you should treat yourself special by caring and nurturing yourself inside and outside. Living your life righteously will help you to achieve all of your hopes and dreams. Additionally, you will become a fantastic mother and wife in the future because you will know what it takes to truly GET YOUR GROWN WOMAN ON!

God loves you, your parents love you, I love you, and please don't forget to love yourself!

Notes

_____

_____

_____

_____

_____

_____

_____

_____

_____

_____

_____

_____

_____

_____

_____

_____

_____

CRYSTAL MORRIS-NEWSOM, MBA

Notes

_____

_____

_____

_____

_____

_____

_____

_____

_____

_____

_____

_____

_____

_____

_____

_____

_____

Notes

CRYSTAL MORRIS-NEWSOM, MBA

REFERENCES

American Academy of Child & Adolescent Psychiatry. (2008).
    Retrieved on March 16, 2011
    http://www.aacap.org/cs/root/facts_for_families/teen_suicide

Suicide prevention, Awareness & Support. (2001).
    Retrieved on March 9, 2011
    www.suicide.org/suicide-statistics.html

About the Author

CRYSTAL R. MORRIS-NEWSOM was born and raised on the southside of Phoenix, Arizona which is where she currently resides with her husband, two sons, and newborn daughter. She loves reading and writing but her other love is medicine. She sold her business and stopped working in the corporate arena to write full time. She graduated from Grand Canyon University with a BS in Human Biology and a minor in Behavioral Science. She graduated for the University of Phoenix with her MBA. Crystal is also a licensed and practicing real estate agent in Phoenix under her grandfather Obadiah Jackson of Obadiah Realty.

After having her daughter she decided it was time to publish the book she had been working on for years for young ladies to read and hopefully gain insight. Sometimes it takes hearing something from someone else to make you understand the reality of what is being said. Her goal is to begin a mentoring program for teen girls to challenge them to think before they act and care for themselves inside and outside. She is dedicated to the encouragement of positive mental development and self love which is lacking in today's society.

Please visit Crystal at *www.crystalnewsom.com* to view upcoming books, book signings in your area, and to sign up for her newsletter.